© Co

MW01224724

UFF DA JOKES

by E.C. "Red" Stangland

published by
NORSE PRESS
Box 1554
Sioux Falls, SD 57101
U.S.A.

**Illustrated by
Don Steinbeck**

ISBN 0-9602692-4-X

Eighth Printing

For more copies of "UFF DA JOKES", send $3.00
(PPD) per copy to:

> NORSE PRESS
> P.O. Box 1554
> Sioux Falls, SD 57101

> Ask For FREE Brochure

UFF DA! MORE THAN AN EXPRESSION

If you come from a Scandinavian family, Uff Da is a familiar expression . . . especially if you have Norwegian ancestry. Uff Da defies precise definition because it has denoted, through ancient custom, a feeling of consternation. Anything from disappointment, sudden pain, suprised reactions to unexpected conditions . . . all may be taken care of with the simple expression "Uff Da." Uff Da is more than an expression . . . it is also a philosophy that one doesn't have to swear, talk dirty, or blow a gasket. Uff Da gives the signal that things are out of control for the moment, but if you will just utter the expression, somehow you will surmount the problem at hand. So, we have adopted the term Uff Da for this book of jokes . . . because the many boo boos and dumb miscues that afflict all of us from time to time can be handled better by not going all to pieces. Just say "Uff Da" and somehow you can muddle through. Norwegians especially have been the target of many terrible but awfully funny jokes, many of which make Norwegians look quite simple. But don't let a Scandinavian's acceptance of these jokes fool you . . . they simply don't take them personally because they are confident that they are nobody's fool. But, perhaps if you THINK they are a bit dumb, they often take advantage and get the best of the deal. So, have a few laughs on us Scandinavians and we'll laugh right along with you. If we get excited, the strongest expression you hear will probably be UFF DA.

Red Stangland, FBN*
(*Full Blooded Norsky)

Red Stangland is the author of over a dozen joke books that have received world-wide circulation. Red is a businessman turned joke writer who has sold over 1,000,000 copies of UFF DA JOKES and several other titles.

A Danish lady sent her husband downtown to get a pair of
loafers. So, he came back with two Norwegians.

> A Swede in our town was never able to develop a liking for
> Norwegians. So, one of his fellow Swedes was surprised
> one day to see the Swede give a coin to a monkey perched
> on the instrument of a Norwegian organ grinder. "I thought
> you didn't like Norwegians," said the friend.
>
> "Yah, dat's true," replied the Swede. "But dey are so
> cute vhen dey are little."

Did you hear about the 900 Norwegians that committed
suicide? They were trying to keep up with the Joneses.

> Ole says: "Da vorst part about being over da hill is dat you
> don't remember ever being on TOP of it."

A Swede in our town invented the phrase, "Don't drink and
drive. You don't know how hard it is to steer and throw up
at the same time."

> Ole doesn't think a lot of the family next door. The father
> writes books that nobody wants to read. The mother writes
> songs that nobody wants to sing. And the son writes
> checks that nobody wants to cash.

SWEDE: Why do they bury Norwegians 12 feet down?
  DANE: I dunno. Why is it?
SWEDE: Becoss... down deep dey are really good people.

> Ole is a born wit. Whenever somebody says, "Well.......",
> Ole always cracks: "Pretty important thing on a farm, ain't
> it?"

When Little Ole's Grandpa came to visit, Little Ole took him aside and asked if he still played football. Grandpa, puzzled, asked what made him think he was a football player. Little Ole answered, "Becoss, my papa says ve're going to get a lot of money vhen you kick off."

Ole got into an argument at the neighborhood bar. Ole was getting a bit excited and started using words he didn't necessarily know the meaning of. The other guy snorted and said, "Ole... I don't want to argue with you. You're ILLITERATE!"

Indignantly, Ole exploded, "Now, you listen here... it so happens my folks vere married ven I vas born."

A Swede received his draft notice and was told to bring a urine sample to the Selective Service Headquarters. Figuring on outfoxing the draft board, the Swede filled a bottle with urine from his father, girlfriend and dog, plus some of his own. After turning in the sample, the Swede waited for about a half hour. The lab technician came out to tell him: "According to our lab test, your father has diabetes, your girlfriend is pregnant, your dog is in heat, and YOU'RE in the Army."

SWEDISH GIRL: "Have your ever been picked up by the fuzz?"
NORWEGIAN GIRL: "No, but I'll bet it hurts."

A roving TV reporter asked Rasmus, "To what do you attribute your old age?"

Answered Rasmus: "Da fact dat I vas born in 1897 probly has sumpting to do vid it."

Why don't Norwegians swat flies? It's their national bird.

Ole got back from a convention in Des Moines and wasn't at all pleased with his hotel room. The noisy people in the next room kept him awake all night.

"Yah," said Ole, "I tink dey vas fighting over candy bars. All night long dis voman kept yelling 'O Henry!!! O Henry!!!'"

While Ole was out by the road checking the mailbox, a car pulled up and the driver asked how to get to Pelican Lake. Ole leaned into the passenger window and said, "First you go up to da corner, turn left and go north two miles. Den you go east for a mile. Den you go north anudder mile and vest for three miles. From dere you go south two miles, east vun mile, south anudder mile, and den east for vun more mile."

Twenty minutes later, the same car pulled into the farmyard, by which time Ole was relaxing on the porch. The driver yelled at him, "Hey, you stupid so-and-so! You just brought me back where I started from!"

Said Ole, "Vell, first I had to see if you could follow directions."

5

SIMPLE NORWEGIAN JIG SAW PUZZLE
(ONE PIECE)

COMPLICATED NORWEGIAN
JIG SAW PUZZLE (2 PIECE)

(Phone rings)
  Ole: Sure is. (hangs up)
Lena: Who vas it?
  Ole: I don't know. Somevun said, "Long distance from
       New York." So I says, "Sure is."

> Why hasn't there been a Norwegian president in the U.S.?
>   --Because they are expected to take a shower before
>   the inauguration.

Ole's mother-in-law had come to stay with Ole and Lena for
an extended visit, and brought her Chihuahua along. The
task of walking the dog every day fell to Ole. One hot
afternoon he got the urge to stop at a cafe for some ice
cream. Since there was no place to tie up the dog outside,
he decided to take it into the cafe. If anyone complained,
he would just say it was a seeing-eye dog. The proprietor
approached Ole and said, "I'm sorry, Sir, but we don't allow
dogs in here."

    "Vell," said Ole, "dis yust happens to be a seeing-eye
dog."

    "I wasn't aware that Chihuahuas were used as seeing-
eye dogs," challenged the man.

    Said Ole: "Dey gave me a Chihuahua?"

> Englishman: Yes... we have only the finest furniture here
> in our castle. For example, that beautiful hand made bed
> goes back to Louis the Fourteenth.
> Ole: Vell, I'm in about da same boat. If ve don't make a
> payment, our furniture goes back to Sears da fifteenth.

Man: (watching a funeral procession)   "Who died?"
Dane: "I tink it vas da guy in da casket."

7

NORWEGIAN ADJUSTABLE DOG CARRIER

A Swede joined a chain letter club. At last report, he had received 579 chains.

Why does it take 15 Norwegians to milk a cow?
--Four to hang on to the faucets, and 11 to move the cow up and down.

Did you hear about the Finn who received a boomerang for his birthday? He went crazy trying to throw the old one away.

A man approached a Norwegian minister about conducting a funeral service for his pet dog. The minister was indignant. "Why, the very idea of asking an ordained minister of the gospel to preach a funeral for a dog!"

The man shrugged and said, "Well, that's a shame you can't do it, because I figured on donating $10,000 to the church that would help me out."

"Well," exclaimed the minister, "why didn't you TELL me it was a LUTHERAN dog?"

A Norwegian went back to Norway after his first trip to the U.S.A. He was describing his experience to friends: "Vell, vhen I first got off da plane, I valked down do street past a shursh, and dey vas singing a song to me: 'Ole, Ole, Ole.' Den I vent to California and my cousin took me to Tijuana to see a bull fight. Dey musta recognized me dere, too, 'cause about every five minutes da crowd vould stand up and yell, 'Ole'... Ole'... Ole'...' But da strangest part about being in America is dat dose folks can't make up dere mind about anyting. You go to shursh and da folks all sing, "Stand up, Stand up for Yesus." Den you go to da ball game and everyone yells, 'For Christ's sake, sit down!' "

The Norwegian government recently purchased 1,000 used septic tanks; and as soon as they learn how to drive them, they plan to invade Sweden.

We know a Finn who's so dumb that he thinks a can opener is a key to the bathroom.

DANE: What would you do if you found a million dollars?
SWEDE: Vell, if it belonged to a poor person, I'd return it.

Ole received a notice in the mail from his employer that he was being laid off from his job. The boss was surprised a few days later to see Ole at the factory gate. "Ole," he said, "I thought I sent you a notice that you were laid off."

"Yah, dat's right boss... but on da envelope it says, 'Return in Five Days to Yohnson's Pickle Factory.' So here I am."

Ole's doctor told Ole he should play 36 holes a day... so Ole bought himself a harmonica.

Knute Knudson had worked hard and finally accumulated enough money to move into town. So, he ordered a fine large house to be constructed. "And," he told the contractor, "I vant you should put a halo statue in every room."

"What in the Sam Hill is a 'halo statue'?" inquired the contractor.

"Vell, you know, dat's vun of dem gadgets you put in da house, and da bell rings and you run over and pick it up and say: 'Halo. Statue?' "

Why does it take three Swedes to eat a rabbit?
--Because it requires two just to look out for cars.

Knute started a new business... it was the first time for him. As he sat admiring his shiny desk, he noticed someone coming in. So, he busily picked up the phone and acted like he was taking a big order. After finishing the "call" he put down the phone and turned to the visitor, saying "Yes... vhat can I do for you?"

"I'm here to install the phone," answered the man.

A Norwegian, an Irishman and a German were sentenced to be electrocuted. First the Irishman was strapped in the chair and the switch was thrown. Nothing happened, so the Irishman was freed. Same thing happened to the German. As the Norwegian was led into the execution room, the prison guard remarked, "Sure has been a lucky day for those two guys."

Said the Norwegian, "Vell, I should say so, becoss I can see da plug has come out of da socket under da chair."

How can Norwegians distinguish boy sardines from girl sardines?
--They watch to see which can they come out of.

Hjalmar went to see a lawyer about a divorce from his wife, Tina. The lawyer began asking some questions. "What grounds do you have?" he asked.

"Grounds?" said Hjalmar. "Vell, ve got about half an acre vid da house."

"No, I mean do you have a grudge?"

Said Hjalmar, "Ya, ve got a single car grudge back of da house."

The lawyer shook his head and continued, "Well, does she beat you up?"

"No, I usually get up about 6 and she stays in bed til 7."

Getting a bit impatient, the lawyer finally asked, "Is she a nagger?"

"No," answered Hjalmar, "she's yust a Norvegian."

A Dane discovered he had mice in the house, so he set a trap. Being a bit thrifty, he used as bait... a picture of a piece of cheese. When he checked the trap the next morning he found... a picture of a mouse!

Three Norwegians began discussing their preferences in female company. The first one extolled the attractions of Raquel Welch, her curves and such. The second said that only Farrah Fawcett Majors could possibly be the ideal for him. The third Norwegian protested that while Farrah and Raquel had their good points, he would have to say that he'd hold out for Virginia Pippaleeny. His companions snorted, saying they'd never even heard of Virginia Pippaleeny. "Who is she?" they asked. "Vell," said the Norsky..."I read about her in da paper today," as he held up the newspaper headline reading "SIX MEN DIE LAYING VIRGINIA PIPELINE."

A Norwegian was hired to paint the center stripe down the middle of a new highway. The first day he completed 3 miles, two miles the second day, but only one the 3rd day. Noting the difference, the superintendent asked for an explanation. "I dunno," puzzled the Norwegian, "I guess it just kept getting farther to go back to that can of paint."

NORWEGIAN I.Q. TEST

This is one of the most difficult intelligence tests ever devised for Norwegians. Try these 10 questions and see how you compare with the average Norwegian.

For example, here are two of the most complicated intelligence test problems.

1. Connect the dots
   • •
   (No fair asking someone the solution)

2. A smart Norwegian, a dumb Norwegian and Santa Claus started walking toward a $20 bill. Which one got it?

   ANSWER: The dumb Norwegian. The other two are fictional.

13

1

HOW DO YOU GET DOWN OFF AN ELEPHANT?

2

FINISH THIS PICTURE

WHO IS BURIED IN GRANT'S TOMB?
- A. George Washington
- B. Millard Fillmore
- C. Abe Lincoln
- D. Ulysses Grant

4

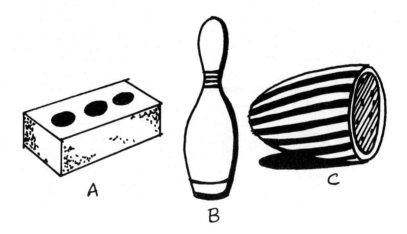

A

B

C

WHICH OF THE ABOVE IS A NORWEGIAN
BOWLING BALL?
 A................
 B. ....
 C. ....

17

WHICH OF THE ABOVE IS A NORWEGIAN SANTA CLAUS?

6

WHAT IS THIS?

7

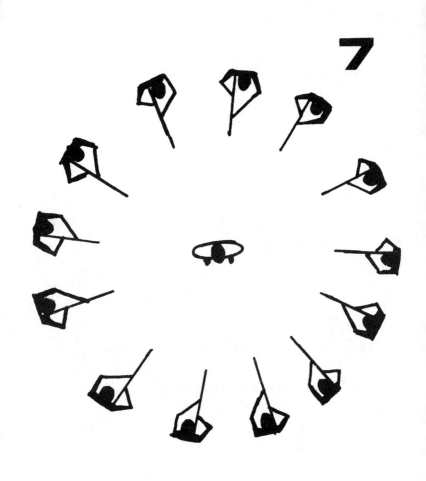

IDENTIFY THIS PICTURE.

8

WHO WAS THE FIRST PRESIDENT OF THE UNITED STATES?
A. Ben Franklin
B. Henny Youngman
C. Harold Stassen
D. George Washington
E. John Hanson

9

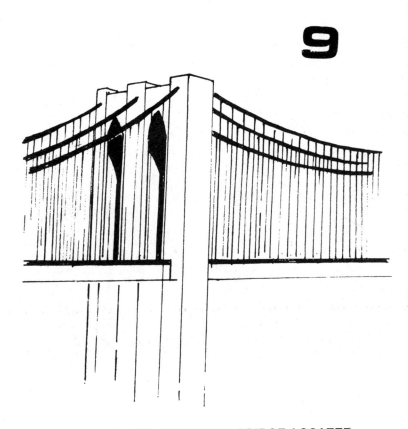

WHERE IS THE BROOKLYN BRIDGE LOCATED:
   A. Hoboken, N. Jersey
   B. Phoenix, Ariz.
   C. Fertile, Iowa
   D. Brooklyn, N.Y.

WHAT DOES THIS PICTURE REPRESENT?

Answers to Norwegian I.Q. Test: 1. You don't get down off an elephant: you get down off a duck. 2. Complete jaw if you can find it. 3. Ulysses Grant. 4. A. 5. The one with an Easter basket. 6. A Norwegian listening to his tapes. 7. Norwegian firing squad. 8. John Hanson. 9. Brooklyn, N.Y. 10. Norwegian listening to the Ink Spots.

An ocean going liner was sailing the Atlantic when it hit an iceberg. Survivors were able to take to lifeboats except one boat that was overloaded by three persons. Nobly, a Frenchman volunteered to sacrifice himself, leaping in the water with a shout, "Vive La France." Next, and Englishman stepped to the edge of the boat, bravely calling out, "God Save the Queen," then jumped into the ocean. Finally, a Norwegian stood up, reached over and grabbed a Swede. He shoved the Swede into the water, and then shouted out, "Long live Norway."

In Suburban Chicago there's a project of neighborhood improvement going on in the Norwegian section. They're building diving boards over the cesspools.

A Swedish barber was cutting a customer's hair when a Norwegian stuck his head in the shop and asked, "How many ahead?" "Two," said the Swede. So the Norwegian disappeared. Next day, same Norwegian, same question: "How many ahead?" "Four," answered the barber. So the Norwegian disappeared again. Next day, same thing. Norwegian asks "How many ahead?" Swedish barber says: "Eight." Again the Norwegian leaves. So the barber told the shoe-shine boy to follow him. Five minutes later the shine boy comes back. "Vell, vere did that crasy Norvegian disappear to?" he asked. "Over to your house," answered the shoe shine boy.

A Swede had been out "on the town" and after too many drinks staggered into the barn to sleep it off. Unknowingly, he settled in with some pigs. When he awoke next morning, he felt a warm body near his back, so he gave a nudge with his elbow, asking, "Er du Svensk?" Answered the pig: "Norsk...Norsk."

"LITTLE NORWEGIAN HOUSE ON THE PRAIRIE"

A Norwegian sat in a bar drinking beer all afternoon. The bartender was getting concerned because the Norwegian hadn't gotten up. Finally, after his 5th pitcher of beer, the Norwegian got up very slowly and headed for the back door. The bartender followed him to the back alley where the Norwegian prepared to relieve himself. "Hey," shouted the bartender, "you can't do that out here."

"I'm not gonna do in HERE," said the Norwegian. "I'm gonna do it waaaaaaay over dere!"

An elderly Norwegian named Lars decided to march to the altar at the ripe age of 85 with a shapely miss who was only 27. His friends cautioned him about the health hazard involved, saying that the exertion of amour could prove to be fatal. "Vell, dat's da chance I'll have to take," said Lars. "If she dies... she dies."

Q: Where do the Swedes keep their armies?
A: Up their sleevies.

A Norwegian was called to the morgue to identify the remains of his friend Olav, who had been in a car accident and decapitated. The coroner took the Norwegian into a room for the identification. The Norwegian held the head rather high in order to get a good look, whereupon he remarked, "Vell, it looks a lot like Olav, but I don't remember him as dis tall a man."

The space program sent a monkey and a Norwegian on a space flight. The monkey's job was to perform certain scientific routines: pushing buttons, pulling levers and so forth. The Norwegian's job was to feed and water the monkey.

Doctor Knudtson walked into the examining room to see Ole. He told him, "I'll have to ask you to fill up that jar on the shelf for me."

A stunned Ole gasped, "From HERE???"

Ole and Lena felt like "getting romantic" on a Saturday afternoon, which was inconvenient because Little Ole was hanging around the house. Ole had an idea. He sent Little Ole out on the front porch and told him to report anything interesting he saw happening in the neighborhood. Ole reminded him, "Yust make sure you yell loud enough so ve can hear you in da house."

Little Ole did as he was told, and started making announcements. "The Yohnsons drove off in their car... A U-Haul truck yust vent by... Somebody came to see da Nelsons... The Torkelsons are having sex..."

Ole jumped out of bed and yelled out the upstairs window, "How do you know dat?"

Little Ole hollered back, "Because dey yust sent Billy Torkelson out on the front porch, too."

Little Ole was practicing his piano lessons, which was putting a strain on Ole's eardrums. "Do you know Mozart wrote fifteen symphonies by da time he vas your age?" snapped Ole.

"Yah, said Little Ole. "And vhen Mozart vas your age, he vas DEAD."

Ole and Lars were out in a boat when a sudden wave caused the boat to sink in three feet of water. Ole immediately reached underwater and pulled on the starter rope four or five times. Lars, looking on, suggested, "Choke it, Ole, choke it!"

THE STORY OF OLE OLSON

Ole Olson was the janitor in the First Lutheran Church in Minneapolis. A new minister decreed that all employees should be able to read and write English. The reasoning was that all employees should be able to handle phone calls and write down information for the minister in his absence. Poor Ole! He had left Norway in his youth and never had learned to read and write. Despite his tearful pleas to the minister, Ole was forced to leave his job as Janitor because of his lack of education.

In his bitter disappointment, Ole hitch hiked to Seattle and got a job in a fish cannery. No worry about reading and writing here. He later worked on a fishing boat, and in time saved enough to buy his own boat.

As time passed, Ole acquired many more boats...in fact, a fishing fleet. With pyramiding profits and Ole's natural thrift, Ole eventually became owner of a small fish cannery in addition to his sizeable fleet of boats.

Then came the opportunity to buy a much larger cannery in Seattle. For the first time in his life, Ole was forced to consider going to a bank because the amount involved was much more than he could handle from his cash reserves.

As Ole recited his list of impressive assets, the banker smiled and assured Ole the loan would be granted. The loan papers were handed to Ole to sign. Said Ole, "I'm sorry...but I don't know how to read or write."

The astounded banker looked at Ole in disbelief. "Mr. Olson...it is necessary for you to sign to make this loan legal. I am astounded at your assets. Just where would you be today IF you could read and write?"

"Vell," said Ole, "I'd probably be a yanitor in the Lutheran Church in Minneapolis."

Authorities have now definitely identified and confirmed the existence of ''Bigfoot.'' It turned out to be a Norwegian wearing four-buckle overshoes.

What did they call the Swede who was half Indian? ''Running Dummy.''

NORSKY FROM MINN'OPLIS

Norskies don't smoke no pot in Minneapolis
A place vere even Svedes can have a ball
Ve fill up on lutefisk and lefse
And snoose is da biggest treat of all.

Ve don't make no trouble vid da Irish
And da Polish people say ve're number vun
Ve let da Viking team fight all our battles
Vile ve take part in all da tailgate fun

I'm proud to be a Norsky from Minnapolis
A place where even Svedes can do their ting
Drinking beer and smoking ol' Bull Durham
And vatching how dat Hennepin can sving.

Dat Bud Grant feller may not be a Norsky
But he's a reg'lar viking yust the same
He took a bunch of rookies to da stadium
And teached dem how to play dat football game.

And I'm proud to be a Norsky from Minneapolis
A place where even Svedes can get along
Vunce a munth we go to Sons of Norvay
An' ve say ''Uff Da'' ven da Tvins go wrong.

Vunce a munth ve go to Sons of Norvay
In Minnoplis, Minnesota, U.S.A.

On a Viking ship the First Mate made this announcement: "I've got some good news and some bad news. First the good news. Today, you will all get some fine hand lotion. Now the bad news. The Captain wants to go water ski-ing today."

LUTEFISK TRAVEL BUREAU
Trip to Norway
June 6 to July 31
12 days and 4 nights

VISIT OSLO, NORWAY
with side trips to Stockholm, Copenhagen and Poland

ITINERARY

1st Day---Leave Twin Cities International Airport---3:30 a.m. Passengers travel sixth class on convertible Lutefisk transport-Passenger carrier single engine Dumbo jet powered by Norwegian corn cobs.

2nd Day---In Air

3rd Day---In Air

4th Day---In Air

5th Day---In Air-Arrive Oslo at 9 p.m. Transfer to Olso YMCA Hilton basement ballroom for Lutefisk-Helper banquet.

6th Day---After breakfast of pickled herring a la mode, all tourists will depart on a complete tour of Oslo from 9:30 to 9:40 a.m. Free time for shoplifting until meeting with the Norwegian "MY FAULT" Insurance Society. We will be entertained in style by local beauties if any can be found. Lunch will be a 7 course meal (a ring of baloney and a 6 pack).

7th Day---Side trip to Sweden, Denmark, and Poland. Tour the countryside in the comfort of a rebuilt Polish Army tank. Watch local peasants working, performing interesting native dances, and changing underwear (with each other).

8th Day---Back to Olso for tour of the University of Norway (both buildings). Everyone will get to see the book in the Health Science Library.

9th Day---Aboard your waiting Dumbo Jet for U.S.A. Only three quick stops. (Two for fuel, and 1 to ask directions.)

10th Day---In Air

11th Day---In Air
12th Day---In Air-   Arrive Twin Cities sometime
          between 9 a.m. and Midnight, depending
          on weather conditions and fuel leakage.
          Custom clearance is quick--no duty on
          Norwegian goods.

Tour cost: $48.50 per couple

Don't delay--Complete coupon reservations. Must be
received **no later** than departure time.

> Please reserve ...... places on the "Trip to Norway".
> Enclosed is my check for $2.04 deposit.
>
> Name ....
> Address ....
> Next of kin ....
> Percent of Norwegian blood ....
>   (Do not go over 100%.)

NORWEGIAN SNOW BLOWER

A Norwegian drove in front of the Cadillac agency in a brand new Cadillac. "Where's your service department?" he asked.

"Service department?" exclaimed the dealer. "You have a brand new Cadillac. You don't need service on it yet, surely?"

"Vell," said the Norwegian. "Ay been used to da stick shift...and this car has got those funny letters like PRNDL on the steering veel."

"Yes, that's correct," said the dealer. "That's the automatic transmission."

"Vell," said the Norwegian. "I first put 'er in 'L' for 'light out.' Den I see a guy trying to pass. So I put 'er in 'S' for 'Sic 'em.' Dat put me a little faster. So when anodder car starts to pass, I looks at the dial and put 'er in 'D' for 'Dig in.' Boy, I really got going. All of a sudden a kid in a hot rod started to go 'round me. So I looked at the dial again and put it in 'R' for 'Racing'."

"Where's your service department?"

A Swede in Minnesota decided to have himself cloned and the result was a perfect likeness of himself in every detail except one. And that was the Clone had a filthy mouth...making obscene remarks wherever he went, much to the extreme embarrassment of the Swede. Finally, it had such a damaging effect on the Swede's life with the rotten-talking Clone ruining his reputation that the Swede invited the Clone to go on an outing to the countryside.

The Swede enticed the clone to view the magnificent scenery from the edge of a cliff, or bluff as they are called in Minnesota. As the Clone leaned forward to glimpse the panorama below, the Swede quickly bumped him from behind and the Clone fell over the 120 foot precipice to the rocks below. When the Swede surmised that death had occurred, he got in his car and went back to town. Several days went by and he figured that when the body was found, it would be presumed an accident with no blame toward him. But one day two policemen walked in and arrested the Swede. Why? For making an obscene Clone fall.

In our town there is a Norwegian who found himself locked in his car, and had to break three windows before he could get out.

A Dane stopped a taxicab in Chicago and asked the driver, ''Do you have room for a six pack of beer and a pizza?'' ''Yeh, buddy, sure do,'' said the Cabby. So the Dane threw up in the back seat.

COACH: Ole, we're short on players. Do you think you can pass this football?''

OLE: ''Yah, Coach, I tink I can if I can svallow it.''

We know a Swede in our town who's a real go getter. His wife has a steady job and at quitting time, the Swede will go getter.

34

Dear Olaf:

How are tings in Visconsin? Ve are all fine here in Minnesota except for Uncle Thorvald. He vas in the hospital vith a veak back. I asked him ven he got a veak back, and he says, "about a veek back." I could tell ven he started getting better becoss he started blowing the foam off the medicine.

I yust got a letter from our brudder in the old country. I can keep it only two days more because it says on the envelope, "return in 5 days."

Our neighbor, Rasmus Johnson died suddenly last veek after being sick for 14 years.

Our old friend, Ole Hanson was lucky last veek. He was held up and killed for his money. He didn't have the money on him so all he lost vas his life.

Early last spring I bought a pig for $5; and two veeks ago I sell him for the same amount. I didn't make any money but I had the use of the pig all summer.

I'm yust getting used to this fancy living in Minnesota...it sure isn't like the old country. Ve got a new barbecue and it seems so different from Norvay...now ve eat outside and go to the bathroom INSIDE.

Emil Krogstad is in poor health. He asked Cousin Bjarne if he vould pour a bottle of viskey over his grave if he should die vun of these days. Bjarne said, "Yah...but vould you mind if I passed it through my kidneys first."

Our neighbor Sven Sandvik has a girl who vants to go to college at the normal school. But Sven von't let her go now because he heard that at that school the boys and girls matriculate together and use the same curriculum. Of course Sven vouldn't stand for dat kinds monkeyshines.

Our Uncle Bertel vent to the bank last veek and asked for a loan. The girl asked if he vanted to see da Loan Arranger. Bertel said he vas in dere for money...he didn't care if da Loan Ranger and Tonto and Silver ver all in town...yust come up with da cash.

Little Arnie yust came home from school and tells me about Abraham Lincoln. I figure dat Abe must be Jewish because little Arnie tells me he vas shot in da temple. As I remember from school, Abe vas born in a log cabin dat he built vith his own two hands. And he did his homevork with a burned stick on the back of a shovel. And what made it tough vas dat he vas taking correspondence school and he had trouble sending in da homevork.

I must go now becoss Kojak is going to be on telewishion with a hair raising story.

Your brudder

Knute

A Norwegian got married and on the wedding night his bride disrobed and suggested, "Get aboard, Ole." By the time Ole got back from the lumber yard, the bride had fallen asleep.

Tena: "Ven are you getting married, Lena?"

Lena: "I'm in no hurry...dere is plenty of fish in da ocean."

Tena: "Yah, dat's right, but your bait is getting stale."

A Danish couple decided to get a divorce because of incompatability. He's lost his income, and she had lost her pat-ability.

Swede: When is your birthday?
Norwegian: March 21st.
Swede: What year?
Norwegian: Every year.

Judge: You've been brought here for drinking.
Dane: Swell! Let's get started.

A Norwegian sent his son to college. In his second year the boy got a girl in trouble. The fast thinking lad wrote to his dad, saying that a professor at the school could teach old Shep to talk for $1,000. Impressed, the Norwegian sent the money and shipped old Shep to the boy. A few months later, the boy committed the same indiscretion, so he wrote the old man again with the claim that the same professor could teach old Shep to read. Again the old man came through with $1,000, feeling that a talking dog should be able to read. At the close of the school year, the Norwegian went to the depot to meet his son coming in on the train. Lo and behold, THERE was the boy...but no old Shep! "Where's old Shep, Son?" asked the father. Again, the fast thinking boy had an answer. "Ya know, Dad, two nights ago old Shep and I were having a chat while he was reading the paper. I said it sure would be good to come back home, and Shep said, yeh, he missed the folks and farm. And he said he wondered if the old man was still fooling around with the hired girl. And you know, Dad, I got so mad at that remark that I reached over and choked that old dog. Before I could control myself, old Shep had died."
Quickly the father leaned forward and asked anxiously, "Are you sure that dog is dead, Son?"

Eye Doctor: "Have your eyes ever been checked?"
Dane: "No...they've always been blue."

The Swede called on his girl friend and his shirt was dripping wet. When asked why he replied, "The label said 'Wash and Wear'."

NORWEGIAN PEEPING TOM

INQUIRING REPORTER: What do you think of the Indianapolis 500?

NORWEGIAN: Vell, I tink dey're all guilty.

SAME INQUIRING REPORTER: What do you think of Red China?

DANE: If you have a yellow table cloth, it should look all right.

A Norwegian in Westby, Wisconsin had a brother in Grand Forks, N. Dak., who passed away. He made arrangements with another brother in Fargo to take care of the burial and then send him the bills for half the expense. So shortly a bill arrived for $100. The Norwegian figured that covered half the funeral so he sent a check. Then a bill for $75 and he figured that was half the casket, so he sent another check. Then a bill for $22.50 which he surmised was to pay for flowers, cemetery plot, etc. A week later, another bill for $22.50. He let that bill lay for a few days and then the next week another bill for $22.50. This mystified the Norwegian in Wisconsin so he picked up the phone and called his brother in Fargo. "I figured out da first bills for funeral, casket and all dat...but vat in da vorld is dis $22.50 dat keeps coming in every veek?" he asked. Answered the brother in Fargo, "Vell, you know Ole didn't have no suit to be buried in, so I vent out and rented him a tuxedo."

Why don't Swede's eat M & M's?
Because they're too hard to peel.

Why do they call Danes such good "do-it yourselfers?"
Because every time their wives ask them to do something, they answer, "Do it yourself."

OLE SAYS YOU KNOW
IT'S GOING TO BE A BAD DAY WHEN...

✓ You wake up face down on the pavement

✓ You call suicide prevention and they put you on hold

✓ You put your bra on backwards and it fits better

✓ You see a "60 Minutes" news team waiting in your office

✓ Your birthday cake collapses from the weight of the candles

✓ Your son tells you he wishes Anita Bryant would mind
her own business

✓ You want to put on the clothes you wore home
from last night's party — and there aren't any

✓ You turn on the news and they're showing emergency
routes out of the city

✓ Your twin sister forgets your birthday

✓ You show up for work, and your boss tells you not to bother
taking off your coat

✓ You wake up to discover that your waterbed broke
and then realize you don't have a waterbed

✓ Your horn goes off accidentally and remains stuck as you follow a
group of Hell's Angels on the freeway

A game warden caught Ole in the act of eating a bald eagle that he had roasted over a fire, and promptly hauled him off to court. Asked to explain why he was eating a bald eagle, Ole told the judge, "Vell, I vas out in da middle of novhere and had nutting to eat. If I hadn't shot dat eagle and cooked it right dere on da spot, I vould have starved."

"Well," said the judge, "the bald eagle IS an endangered species, but since you were starving, I guess you can't be blamed for doing what was necessary to stay alive. I find you not guilty."

As Ole was leaving the judge asked, "By the way, what does bald eagle taste like?"

Ole said, "It's sort of a cross between whooping crane and California condor."

Wisdom of Ole: "Money isn't everything... Henry Ford, vid all dat money... millions of dollars... never owned a Cadillac."

Knute Heggermoe wanted to get a special birthday cake for his wife. He called the bakery and gave his order to Lena, who was working there at the time. He specified, "I want it to say 'You're not getting older' on the top, and I want it to say 'You're getting better' on the bottom."

The next day he picked up the cake, which Lena had decorated. When he got it home, he opened the box and found this inscription:

YOU'RE NOT GETTING OLDER ON THE TOP,
YOU'RE GETTING BETTER ON THE BOTTOM.

Ole's nephew Torkel Halvorson was in the Marine Corps. The sergeant asked Torkel why he didn't show up for camouflage class that morning. Torkel replied casually, "Vhat makes you so sure I vasn't dere?"

We heard recently that a Finn broke his shoulder during a pie eating contest. A cow fell on him.

> Ole: My brudder says he's sick.
> Doctor: Now Ole, your brother is hale and hearty. He just THINKS he's sick.
> *Two days later:*
> Doctor: How's your brother?
> Ole: He thinks he's dead.

A plane carrying Jimmy Carter, Gerald Ford, Henry Kissinger, a priest and a Norwegian hippie was crossing the U.S. when it developed engine trouble. The pilot and co-pilot had parachutes and bailed out, informing the others that there were four parachutes left. Seeing that there were five persons left aboard, Jimmy Carter said, "The American people would want their president saved." So, he grabbed one of the parachutes and jumped. Gerald Ford declared that as ex-president, he should also be saved, so he grabbed a parachute, and out the hatch he went.

Henry Kissinger then said, "Since I am da schmartest man in da vorld, I should be saved," so he grabbed a pack and leaped out of the plane.

The priest said, "Well, with only one parachute left, I have decided to stay on the plane. I have had a good life and am at peace with my maker. So I will remain."

"Von't be necessary," said the Norwegian hippie. "Da smartest man in da vorld yust yumped out vid my back pack."

OLE SAYS... YOU KNOW YOU'RE GETTING OLD WHEN...

✓ Everything hurts and what doesn't hurt, doesn't work

✓ The gleam in your eyes is from the sun hitting your bifocals

✓ You feel like the night after, and you haven't been anywhere

✓ Your little black book contains only names ending in M.D.

✓ You get winded playing chess

✓ Your children begin to look middle aged

✓ A dripping faucet causes an uncontrollable bladder urge

✓ You know all the answers, but nobody asks you the questions

✓ You look forward to a dull evening

✓ Your favorite part of the newspaper is "25 Years Ago Today"

✓ You turn out the light for economic rather than romantic reasons

✓ You sit in a rocking chair and can't get it going

✓ Your knees buckle and your belt won't

✓ You're 17 around the neck, 42 around the waist, and 119 around the golf course

✓ Dialing long distance wears you out

✓ You're startled the first time you are addressed as an old timer

✓ You can't stand people who are intolerant

✓ You burn the midnight oil until 9 P.M.

✓ Your back goes out more often than you do

✓ A fortune teller offers to read your face

✓ Your pacemaker makes the garage door go up when you watch a pretty girl go by

Ole got a new snowmobile, so he and Lars took it to a field out in the country for a tryout. Ole went first, and after a little practice, he decided to open it up full throttle. Unfortunately, the throttle got stuck in the wide open position. Being Scandinavian, he didn't have the presence of mind to shut off the ignition. So, around and around he went at breakneck speed, holding on for dear life to the steering controls. Lars stood there, stunned speechless; there was nothing he could do, and nowhere to run for help. Finally, while trying to take too sharp of a turn, the machine flipped, sending Ole flying. Lars immediately ran to where Ole was lying and pleaded, "Speak to me, Ole! Speak to me!"

"Vhy should I?" moaned Ole. "I passed you six times and you never so much as said 'Hello'."

Mrs. Newlyrich: "Yass, when we were in Frawnce last summah, I went to the Louvre eight times."

Lena: "Hmmmmm... probably vas da vater."

Momma Johnson: Eat your spinach, Hjalmar.
It'll put color in your cheeks.

Hjalmar: Who vants green cheeks?

Ole wanted to sell his old car, but with 92,000 miles on it, he didn't think it would bring a very good price. So, he and Lars fiddled with the odometer and rolled it back to 11,000 miles. A few days later, he met Lars again who asked, "Did you sell dat old clunker yet?"

"I changed my mind," said Ole. "Vhy vould I vant to get rid of a low mileage car like dat?"

What are the happiest five years of a Norwegian's life?
--First grade.

There was a Swede who was so dumb he thought Abraham Lincoln was a Jewish automobile agency.

Pollster: What is your opinion of Yeltsin?
Ole: I don't know. I've never yeltzed.

The manager of a New York nightclub was having trouble finding reliable bouncers. So, finally he decided to use a gorilla, one of which had become available from a bankrupt circus. On the gorilla's first night on the job, who should wander in the door but Ole, fresh off the boat from the Old Country. Ole gets a few drinks in him, and starts singing "Kan du Glemma gamle Norge?" very loudly and very off-key. After the seventeenth verse, the manager decides he's had enough, so he unleashes the gorilla and directs it over to Ole. The gorilla drags Ole out in the alley to work him over. An awful commotion is heard coming from outside: punches, groans, the clatter of garbage cans. Five minutes later Ole walks back in, brushing himself off and readjusting his trousers. He says, "How do you like dat? Dey give a Swede a fur coat and he tinks he owns da place!"

Describe Danish cough medicine: A bottle of Castor oil.
Two spoonfuls and you don't DARE cough.

Insurance Salesman: Now, before we complete this policy, do you want an Ordinary Life?
Ole: Vell, I VOULD like to fool around a little on Saturday night.

45

"O Lutefisk"

[May be sung to the tune of "O Tannenbaum"]

O Lutefisk... O Lutefisk... how fragrant your aroma
O Lutefisk... O Lutefisk... You put me in a coma.
You smell so strong... you look like glue
You taste yust like an overshoe
But Lutefisk... come Saturday
I tink I'll eat you anyvay.

O Lutefisk... O Lutefisk... I put you by the door vay
I vanted you to ripen up... yust like dey do in Norvay
A dog came by and sprinkled you... I hit him vid an army shoe
O Lutefisk... now I suppose
I'll eat you as I hold my nose.

O Lutefisk... O Lutefisk... how vell I do remember
On Christmas eve how we'd receive... our big treat of December
It vasn't turkey or fried ham... it vasn't even pickled spam
My mudder knew dere vas no risk...
In serving buttered lutefisk.

O Lutefisk... O Lutefisk... now everyone discovers
Dat Lutefisk and lefse makes... Norvegians better lovers
Now all da vorld can have a ball... you're better dan dat Yeritol
O Lutefisk... vid brennevin
You make me feel like Errol Flynn.

There's even MORE fun waiting when you order from the book list below.

	Price	Qty.	Total
* Polish Jokes	$3.00		
* Norwegian Jokes	$3.00		
* Uff Da Jokes	$3.00		
* More Uff Da Jokes	$3.00		
* Ole & Lena Jokes 1	$3.00		
* More Ole & Lena Jokes 2	$3.00		
* Ole & Lena Jokes III	$3.00		
* Ole & Lena Jokes 4	$3.00		
* Ole & Lena Jokes 5	$3.00		
* Ole & Lena Jokes 6	$3.00		
* Ole & Lena Jokes 7	$3.00		
* Office Jokes (R Rated)	$2.75		
* Blonde Jokes	$2.50		
* Norwegian Book of Knowledge	$1.75		
* Swedish Book of Knowledge	$1.75		
(Above two titles have blank text and humorous material on back cover)			
*O Lutefisk (Nostalgia ... growing up during the Depression in a small town)	$8.95		
* How to Become Your Own Boss ... Shortcuts on becoming self-employed	$4.95		
	GRAND TOTAL		

ALL PRICES INCLUDE POSTAGE AND HANDLING
10% DISCOUNT ON ORDERS OVER $15.00

Name _____

Address _____

_____

Send cash, check or money order to:
NORSE PRESS, Box 1554, Sioux Falls, SD 57101